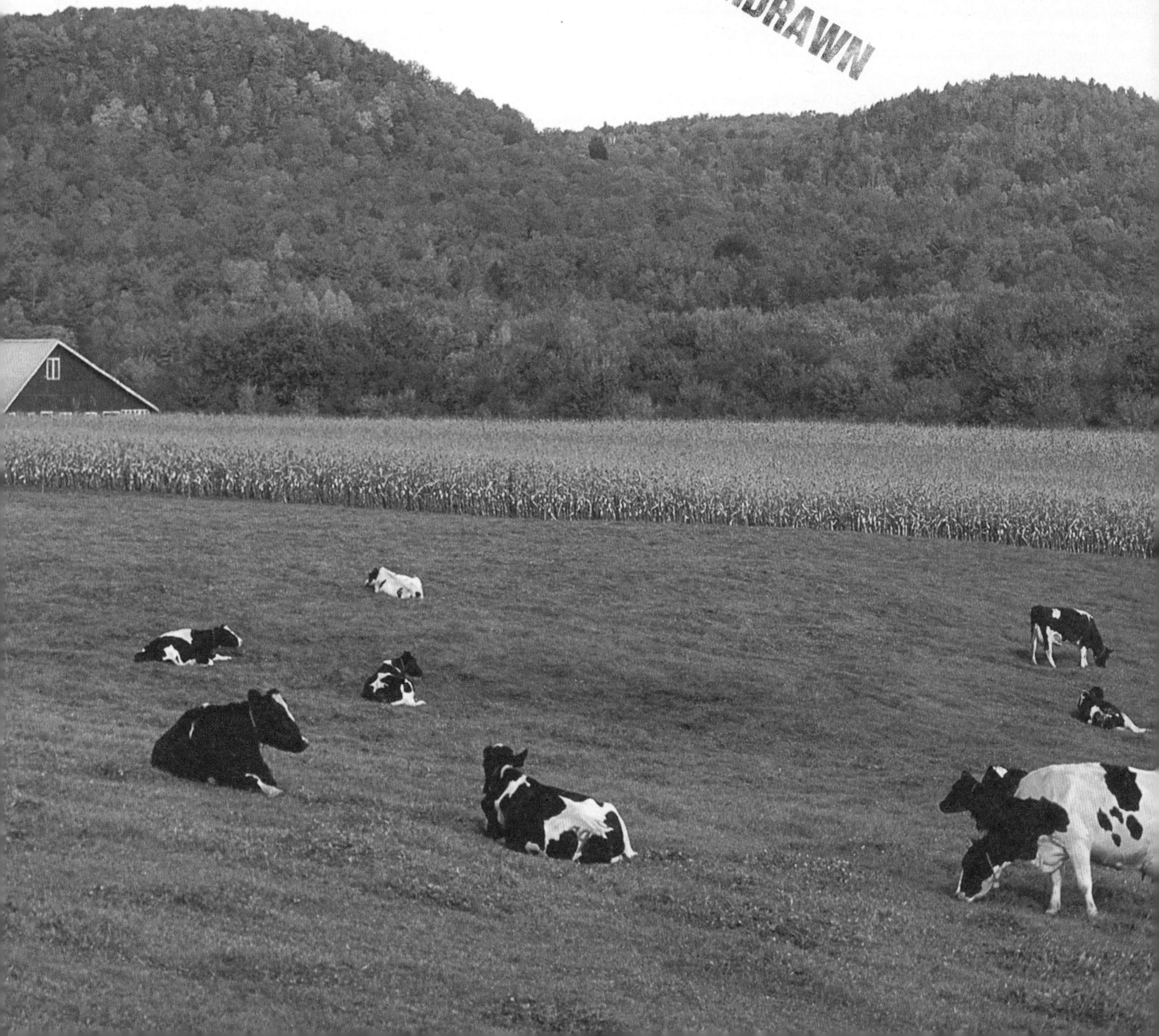

ALL AROUND THE FARM

JOHN DEERE

ALL AROUND THE FARM

By Heather Alexander

DK

DK Publishing

PARACHUTE PRESS   JOHN DEERE
LICENSED PRODUCT

LONDON, NEW YORK, MUNICH,
MELBOURNE, and DELHI

Associate Editor Alisha Niehaus
Senior Editor Elizabeth Hester
Design Jessica Park
Managing Art Editor Michelle Baxter
Publishing Director Beth Sutinis

Book Designer Greg Wozney
Associate Designer Annemarie Redmond

Special thanks to Carol Clement,
Heather Ridge Farm, Preston Hollow, NY

Published in the United States by
DK Publishing
375 Hudson Street
New York, New York 10014

07 08 09 10 11 10 9 8 7 6 5 4 3 2 1

Created and produced by
Parachute Publishing, L.L.C.
322 Eighth Avenue
New York, NY 10001

A catalog record for this book is
available from the Library of Congress.

ISBN-13: 978-0-7566-2977-9
ISBN-10: 0-7566-2977-2

Printed in China by Imago

Discover more at
www.dk.com

Contents

The farm

Did you know that the cereal you eat for breakfast, the peanut butter in your sandwich, and even your favorite blanket come from a farm? Farmers work hard to produce the things that you eat and use every day. Some farms grow plants, which are called **crops**. Some farms raise animals, which are called **livestock**. Some farms do both. You can find many different kinds of farms in all corners of the world.

Farm machines

Farmers often use powerful **machines**, like this tractor, to help with their work on the farm.

Farmers

Farmers do many different kinds of work. If you were a farmer, this is how your day might go.

Around the clock job

Farmers wake up at dawn when the rooster crows, ready for a full day's work.

5:00 A.M.	Milk the cows.
7:00 A.M.	Feed the animals and bring them to pasture.
9:00 A.M.	Collect the eggs from the hen house.
11:00 A.M.	Harvest the fields.
3:00 P.M.	Repair a broken fence.
5:00 P.M.	Milk the cows again.
7:00 P.M.	Bring the animals into the barn for the night.
8:00 P.M.	Continue harvesting the fields.
10:00 P.M.	Nurse a sick calf.

What do farmers do?

✔ Learn all about farming so that they can choose the crops and livestock that are best for their land.

✔ Give their crops and livestock the right amount of food and water to keep them strong and healthy and protect them from pests and diseases.

✔ Find the best way to deliver their farm products to people who want to buy them.

✔ Protect the soil, air, and water so that they remain safe and healthy for today and for future generations.

Did You Know?

You can grow up to be a farmer even if you don't live on a farm. There are many ways to learn about farming. One way is to go to agricultural college, where you can study farm animals, crops, and healthy soil.

Planting
This farmer plants the seeds in rows.

Almost ready
This farmer checks his crop.

Teamwork
These farmers work together for a successful harvest.

Kids on the farm

Growing up on a farm means there's always lots to do. And often, kids on a farm help out. Kids can have fun feeding the baby animals, and watching them grow. Kids may also help weed and water vegetable gardens.

Feeding animals
This girl feeds and gives water to a calf.

A small job
Even young children can help. This boy feeds the tiny chicks.

A big job

Hay bales are too heavy for the younger children to lift, so older kids might help out by bringing fresh hay to the animals in the barn.

Exercise

Horses need exercise every day. Kids can help by taking them out for a walk or a ride.

Farm competitions

Many kids work all year to get ready for livestock and crop competitions. Some raise goats, chickens, or pigs to be judged. Other kids grow vegetables, fruits, or plants. And some bake fruit pies or knit scarves from sheep's wool for the competition. The winner goes home with a blue ribbon.

Did You Know?

It's fun to visit a farm. You can pick apples, pumpkins, or other kinds of fruit and vegetables. Or you can take a hay ride.

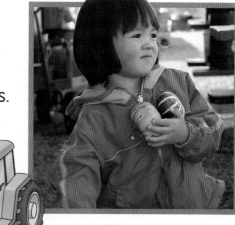

lemons

apples

carrots

raspberries

Crops

There are many kinds of crops grown on farms. Some crops are foods we eat. Vegetables, fruit, and grain are crops that we eat. Some crops become things that we wear. Cotton is a crop that we wear. What kind of crop did this book come from? If you said trees, you're right. Paper is made from the wood we get from trees.

What do crops need?

Good soil

Crops need good soil to grow. Some farmers **rotate** their crops to improve the soil. By changing the type of plant grown on the land, the farmer gives the soil a chance to replenish lost **nutrients**, or vitamins.

Hay is an important crop. It is used to feed animals.

wheat

cotton

corn

peppers

The right weather

The weather is very important for crops. Plants need sunshine and the right temperature at the right time. A heat wave or an early or late freeze can wipe out a crop.

Water

Crops need to get the right amount of water. Too little rain causes a **drought**. Too much rain causes a **flood**. Both a drought and a flood can destroy crops. Farmers can't always wait for a rainstorm, so they **irrigate**—or water—their fields with sprinklers and special irrigation machines.

Did You Know?

Farmers choose the crops they plant based on the length of the growing season—the time from the last frost in Spring to the first frost in Fall—and the **climate**, which is the weather over a long period of time. Different crops grow better in different climates. Wheat, rice, and citrus fruit grow better in a warm climate. Corn and potatoes grow better in a cooler climate.

irrigation machine

Plants

Fruits, vegetables, grains, and fibers are just some of the crops that come from plants. Plants are like you, because they are living things, and they need food, water, sunlight, and air to grow.

The parts of a plant

seeds

Seeds are the smallest part of a plant. If you bury seeds in the ground a new plant will grow.

roots

The roots of a plant grow under the ground. They take in water and nutrients from the soil.

stems

The stem of a plant carries the water and nutrients from the roots to the leaves.

Did You Know?

Tiny seeds contain all the information that a plant needs to grow. A pumpkin seed knows how to grow into a pumpkin plant, a tomato seed knows how to becomes a tomato plant, and an apple seed knows how to become a great big apple tree.

leaves

Plant leaves gather energy from the sun and turn it into food for the plant. This is called photosynthesis.

flowers

Flowers are where the seeds of the plant are found.

From seed to plant

❶ First, the seeds are covered by soil. The soil needs to be healthy and loose enough for air to move through it.

❷ With the right amount of water and warmth, the seed **germinates**, or grows into a very young plant called a **seedling**. The seedling then gets oxygen or air from the soil.

❸ Next, the roots grow and reach deep underground to anchor the plant.

❹ Finally, the stem of the plant pokes up from the soil and grows toward the sunlight. Soon, the seedling will become a strong plant.

Planting the field

Farmers choose the crops they grow very carefully. Some crops grow better in dry soil. Some crops grow better in wet soil. Some crops like a lot of sun. Others like shade better. Farmers also select crops that grow well together. They often plant lettuce and cucumbers, which grow low to the ground, right under tall bean, tomato, or corn plants. The tall crops reach for the sun and, at the same time, help the low crops by giving them shade.

Preparing the soil

Farmers need to turn over a field's soil to loosen it before they plant. This is called **tillage**.

Plow

Many farmers use a **plow** to break up the hard soil and turn it over into **furrows** or rows.

FUN FACT

Plants love garbage. The kind of garbage they like is called **compost**. Compost is made by combining food scraps, plant cuttings, and the leaves that fall from the trees in autumn and letting them all rot together for a long time.

Seeds and seedlings

Some crops are planted by dropping seeds into the soil. Others are planted from seedlings that the farmer starts in a greenhouse.

Planter

The planter drops large seeds, such as corn, into the furrows. The planter then covers the seeds with soil.

Food for plants

Soil might not naturally have the right amount and kind of nutrients that plants need to grow year after year. Farmers help put these nutrients into the soil with **fertilizer**. Fertilizer is packed with vitamins and minerals. Farmers also let old plants **decompose**, or rot, to keep the soil strong and put nutrients back into the earth.

Manure spreader

Organic fertilizer comes from nature. Compost, fruit and vegetable scraps, and **manure**, or animal waste, make good fertilizer. Farmers attach special wagons to tractors to spread natural fertilizer throughout their fields.

Sprayer

Chemical fertilizers are mixed with water, put into tanks, and sprayed over the field.

Protecting the crops

Farmers must protect their crops so they can grow healthy and strong.

Scarecrows

Scarecrows frighten away hungry birds, especially big birds called crows, so they won't eat the newly-planted crops.

cultivator

crop duster

Destroying weeds

Weeds are plants that steal the nutrients in the soil that the crops need to grow. Many farmers control the weeds with chemicals. Another way weeds are destroyed is by cultivating the field. A **cultivator** digs out the weeds. A **hoe** can be used to do the same thing in small gardens.

Did You Know?

Farmers love ladybugs. Thousands of bugs live on a farm. Many bugs, such as aphids, eat the leaves of the crops. Farmers use ladybugs to stop aphids. One ladybug can eat 5,000 aphids!

Pesticides

Some farmers use chemical **pesticides** to keep bugs, worms, mice, and other pests from eating their crops. Airplanes called **crop dusters** fly over large fields and spray pesticides from up in the air.

Organic farms

Some farmers do not use chemical pesticides. They try to use natural ways to protect their crops, such as removing bugs with sticky paper instead of with chemicals. This is called **organic farming**. These farmers label their fruits and vegetables as "organic."

Tractors

A tractor is one of the most important machines on a farm. Tractors come in different sizes so farmers can choose the right tractor for the job. For a big farm, farmers might choose a huge twelve-wheel tractor with lots of power. For a fruit farm, they might choose a small tractor that can drive through narrow rows of fruit trees.

The **back window** opens to let in fresh air.

Big rear tires with heavy treads and deep grooves keep the tractor from getting stuck in mud.

A powerful **engine** lets the tractor pull heavy equipment up steep slopes.

The **cab** is where farmers sit to drive. The cab is up high so the farmer has a good view of the fields.

Headlights allow farmers to work at night or in rain or fog.

Smaller front tires make turning the tractor easy.

JOHN DEERE
tractors through the years
Look how much tractors have changed!

Model D from 1924

Model LA from 1941

Model 7020 from 1971

Tractor attachments

There are lots of different kinds of attachments a farmer can use with a tractor. Some are attached to the front of the tractor and some to the back. All the attachments get their power from the tractor.

Seed drill

This tractor pulls a seed drill. The seed drill makes holes in the soil and then drops seeds deep into them. Then it covers the holes with dirt.

Disk

This tractor is pulling a disk. Disks break up hard soil with heavy blades to get the field ready for planting.

Baler

This tractor pulls a baler. A baler collects hay from the field and wraps it into bales to make moving the hay easier.

Harvester

The tractor below pulls a sugar beet harvester. The harvester separates the leaves and the stalks from the roots of the sugar beet. The roots are sent to factories to make sugar.

Bale fork

The bale fork attaches to the front of the tractor. It is used to lift and carry the bales of hay.

Mower

Cutting the tall grass is easy when a tractor pulls a mower.

The combine

The combine is the largest machine on the farm. Combines harvest **grain**. Wheat, corn, and rice are different kinds of grain.

cutter bar

grain tank

threshing
cylinder

Did You Know?

Years ago, combines were pulled by horses. Later, they were pulled by tractors. Today, combines have powerful engines of their own.

combine control panel

FUN FACT

A combine can harvest enough wheat in nine seconds to make 70 loaves of bread!

Harvesting grain

Harvesting grain is a big job. The farmer uses a **combine** to cut the corn or wheat and separate the grain from the stalks.

combine harvester _____

How combines harvest wheat

❶ The combine first cuts the **stalks** of the plant with the sharp blades of its **cutter bar**.

❷ In the **threshing cylinder** inside the combine, the **grain**—small hard seeds or kernels—is separated from the stalk, cleaned, and placed in a **grain tank**.

❸ The combine leaves the **straw**—the plant's stalk—out on the field. It will be collected later and used in animal pens or turned into pulp for paper.

Pasta
is made from wheat.

Corn harvesting

Combines have a different attachment for harvesting corn.

corn head attachment

corn plant

Did You Know?

Many farms grow two different kinds of corn: feed corn for the farm animals and sweet corn for people to eat.

Tortilla chips

are made from corn.

feed corn

sweet corn

Pizza from the farm

Have you ever seen a pizza plant? Of course not. Pizza doesn't grow in the fields, but all of its ingredients come from the farm.

Crust
The farmer grows **wheat**, which is ground into **flour**. The flour is mixed with yeast and water to make dough for the crust.

Sauce
The farmer grows **tomatoes** and **garlic**, which are crushed and cooked to make sauce. **Herbs** like **parsley** or **basil** may also be added.

Cheese
Dairy cows, goats, and sheep make **milk**, which is made into the cheese on your pizza.

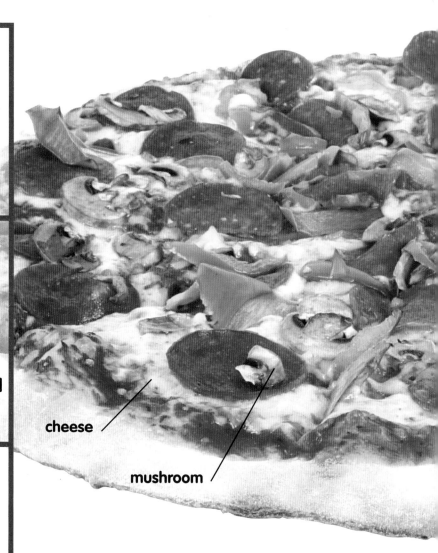

cheese

mushroom

All kinds of toppings come from the farm!

◆ sausage, pepperoni, chicken
◆ peppers, onions, mushrooms, spinach
◆ olives, pineapple, eggplant

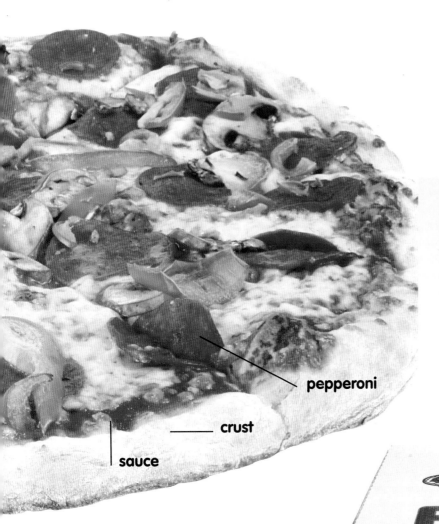

pepperoni

crust

sauce

Did You Know?

Even the box is made from things that grow on farms. Cardboard comes from trees. The glue that holds the box together comes from corn. And the ink for printing the words on the box can come from soybeans.

PIZZA

Vegetables from the farm

Vegetables come from all parts of a plant. Some of the vegetables that you eat are actually the leaves of a plant. Some are the flowers of a plant. And some are the roots, bulbs, or seeds of a plant.

All in a row

Vegetables are planted in long rows. The farmers leave enough room between rows so a tractor can drive through without crushing the vegetables.

Leaves

Lettuce, cabbage, and spinach are plant **leaves**. They grow straight out of the ground.

Flowers

Broccoli, artichokes, and cauliflower are **flowers**. They also grow straight out of the ground.

Roots

Carrots, potatoes, and radishes are **roots**. They grow underground.

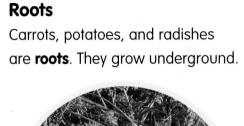

Bulbs

Onions and garlic are **bulbs**. They grow underground, too.

Seeds

Peas and lima beans are **seeds**. They grow on tall vines.

Did You Know?

Vegetables come in all different colors, but they all start out green. As they grow, their true colors develop.

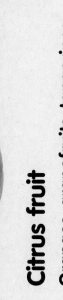

Fruit from the farm

Do you know the difference between a fruit and a vegetable? This is not an easy question. Scientists say a fruit is the fleshy part of a plant that has seeds. They say vegetables come from other parts of a plant, such as the roots, leaves, and flowers. This makes pumpkins, avocados, and tomatoes fruits! Grocers disagree. They say that if the plant is used in a common salad, it is a vegetable. What do you think?

Berries

There are many kinds of berries. Berries grow on bushes and vines. **Strawberries** and **blueberries** are two of the most popular berries.

Citrus fruit

Oranges, grapefruits, tangerines, lemons, and **limes** are citrus fruits. Citrus fruit grows on trees in warm temperatures. A frost can destroy a citrus tree, so many farmers put heaters by their trees to keep them warm! Citrus fruit bruises easily, so it must be picked carefully by hand.

Vineyards

The area where **grapes** are grown is called a **vineyard**. Grapes can be purple, red, green, or white. There are two types of grapes. **Table grapes** are grapes used for eating or making jelly. **Wine grapes** are grapes used to make wine.

FUN FACTs

- Raisins are made from grapes that have been dried.
- The grapefruit got its name from the way it grows in clusters, like grapes.
- The navel orange got its name because the bottom of the fruit looks like a navel, which is another word for bellybutton!

Apple orchards

Apple trees are grown in **orchards**, areas where fruit trees grow. Most apple trees will start to give fruit four to five years after they are planted. Farmers plant the trees in neat rows, just wide enough for a tractor to fit though.

The most popular apples in the United States are:

Red Delicious   Gala   Granny Smith   Fuji   Golden Delicious   McIntosh

Did You Know?

There are 7,500 different kinds of apples grown throughout the world.

Growing an apple

Apple trees blossom in the spring with sweet-smelling white flowers. When the flowers fall off the branches, apples grow in their place.

Ripe and ready

Apples are harvested in the fall. Farmers often use tractors to transport apples from the orchards back to the barn.

How to pick an apple

All apples must be picked carefully by hand so they don't bruise. To pick an apple, twist it on the stem, and it should snap off.

FUN FACT

Apples float because they are 25% air.

The barn

The **barn** is an important building on a farm. It can be used to store farm machines, hay, and saddles for horseback riding. It also protects animals, like horses and cows, from the rain and snow.

Around the barn

Barns come in all different sizes, colors, and shapes. Some barns, like the one below, are round. Round barns are mostly found in the midwestern United States. In the late 1800s and early 1900s, farmers built round barns because they thought they'd hold up better against fierce prairie storms.

Did You Know?

Farmers often have cats that live in the barn to chase away mice that might eat the hay or scare the horses.

Silos

The silo is a tall cylinder that stores **fodder**. Fodder is corn or hay that is chopped up. It is used to feed animals in the winter. Silos are also used to store wheat before the farmer brings it to the market.

Hay

Hay is grass that has been cut and dried in the sun. There are many kinds of grass that can be used to make hay, such as alfalfa, clover, and rye.

Round bales
Each hay bale can weigh up to 1,500 pounds—that's the same as a full-grown cow.

Square bales

Square hay bales are lighter and easier to handle than round bales.

Do you know why school is closed during the summer? Years ago, when most kids lived on farms, students were needed at home during the summer months to help with the harvest.

Feeding animals

Horses, cows, sheep, and goats eat hay. Sometimes farmers feed the animals in the barn, epecially when it is cold or wet outside. Farmers also put hay for the horses outside in the **pasture**.

Horses

One hundred years ago, just about every farm had a horse—and most farms had lots of horses. Farmers had to travel from one end of the farm to the other, and it was much faster to ride a horse than to go by foot. Today, most farmers use tractors and trucks to cross their land—but people still love to ride horses!

A male horse is a **stallion**.
A female horse is a **mare**.
A baby horse is a **foal**.
A young male horse is a **colt**.
A young female horse is a **filly**.
A **pony** is a smaller type of horse.

Horsepower

A tractor's engine is described in terms of **horsepower**. If a tractor has a 250-horsepower engine, that means it has the pulling power of 250 horses.

Gaits

Horses have different ways of moving, called gaits. From slowest to fastest, a horse's **gaits** are: **walk**, **trot**, **canter**, and **gallop**.

Work, work, work

Draft horses are work horses that pull heavy loads. They are different from horses that people ride. They are bred to be strong. Before there were tractors, horses did most of the work on a farm, such as pulling heavy plows and carts.

Did You Know?

A newborn horse can stand up on its own just one hour after being born. It takes a human baby nine to 18 months to stand on its own. After one day, the foal can keep up with the rest of the herd.

Chickens

Did you know that there are more chickens in the world than people? And there are more chickens than any other kind of bird. That's a lot of chickens. Farmers raise chickens for their eggs and their meat.

The **comb** is the red crest on the top of the head.

Wattles are the flaps of skin hanging down from the throat.

Feathers keep the chicken warm. Once a year, chickens **molt**. This means their old feathers fall out and new, healthier ones grow back in.

Female chickens are called **hens**.
Male chickens are **roosters**.
Baby chickens are called **chicks**.

Flocks

Chickens live in groups called **flocks**. In a flock, the stronger birds peck at the other birds in order to get the best food and best place to rest. This is called the **pecking order**.

Brown or white?

Some hens lay brown eggs. Some hens lay white eggs. There are even some hens that lay green or blue eggs. The color of the eggshell depends on the kind, or **breed**, of the hen that laid it.

Did You Know?

Chickens love to eat worms, insects, and weeds. Years ago, farmers would let their chickens out in the fields to clear the land before it was plowed.

Chicks

Why do hens sit on their eggs? It keeps the eggs warm, and eggs need to be kept warm for the chicks to hatch. Some farmers help keep the eggs warm by putting them under special heat lamps. After 21 days, a fluffy little chick will hatch from the egg.

Other farm animals

Pigs

Baby pigs weigh only about three pounds when they are born, but they can grow to weigh more than 800 pounds. Meat from a pig is called **pork**. Ham, bacon, sausage, and pepperoni come from pigs.

A pig that weighs over 125 pounds is called a **hog**.

A male pig is a **boar**.

A female pig is a **sow**.

A baby pig is a **piglet**.

Lots of piglets

A female pig will give birth to a **litter** of 10 or more piglets. She will usually do this twice a year.

Did You Know?

Pigs can't sweat when they get hot like many other animals do. They have no sweat glands. Instead they roll in the mud when they want to cool off.

Goats

Goats are very curious. They'll nibble anything nearby to see if it tastes good—including weeds, garbage, and even clothes. Goats are raised for their milk and for meat.

A male goat is a **billy goat**.

A female goat is a **nanny goat**.

A baby goat is called a **kid**.

FUN FACT

Have you ever tasted the milk that comes from a goat? More children around the world drink goat's milk every day than cow's milk.

Sheep

Sheep grow a thick coat of wool, called **fleece**, on their bodies to keep them warm in the winter. Every spring, sheep are **sheared**, which means their fleece is shaved off. This does not hurt the sheep. The wool is spun into yarn to make clothing and blankets. The sheep grow new coats each year.

A male sheep is a **ram**.
A female sheep is an **ewe**.
A young sheep is a **lamb**.

two lambs

Dairy farm

Where does your milk come from? From cows raised on dairy farms. On a large dairy farm, modern machines can milk more than 300 cows an hour.

Dairy cows

Holstein cows are black and white. They produce the greatest amount of milk. A Holstein's spots are like fingerprints—no two cows have the same pattern.
Jersey cows are light brown. Their milk is high in fat, so it is good for making **butter**, **cheese**, **yogurt**, and **ice cream**.

Holstein cow

Jersey cow

Milking the cow

A cow's milk is stored in her **udder**.
Cows are milked twice a day—in the morning and at night.

udder

From cow to carton

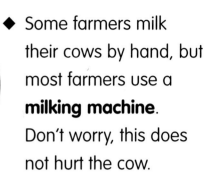

◆ Some farmers milk their cows by hand, but most farmers use a **milking machine**. Don't worry, this does not hurt the cow.

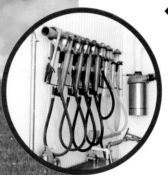

◆ The milk is pumped into a big **milk tank**. The milk is warm when it comes out of the cow, but the tank refrigerates it so it will stay fresh.

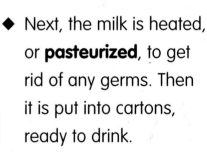

◆ Next, the milk is heated, or **pasteurized**, to get rid of any germs. Then it is put into cartons, ready to drink.

FUN FACT

One cow produces about 200,000 glasses of milk in its lifetime.

Cattle farm

Cattle farms are sometimes called ranches. These are places where cows are raised for beef and leather products.

A baby cow is called a **calf**.
A female cow is called a **heifer**.
A male cow is called a **bull** or a **steer**.

Chewing cud

Cows eat very fast and don't chew their food. Later, they burp up bits of food, called **cud**, and slowly chew them. A cow spends about eight hours a day chewing cud.

No front teeth

When cows **graze**, or eat in the pasture, they must tear at the grass with their lips and gums because they have no front teeth.

Dinner time

This tractor is pulling a **feed wagon**. The feed is placed in **troughs**, or large buckets. Some cows eat only grass, others eat a special mixture of grains, beans, vitamins, and minerals. Each cow eats about 100 pounds of food a day!

The round up

Cattle are kept in large groups called **herds**. Some herds have as many as 1,000 cattle in them. Cowhands on horseback keep all these cows together while they move the herd from pasture to pasture.

FUN FACT

The hide, or skin, of one cow can make 20 leather footballs or 18 leather soccer balls.

Gators™

The **Gator**™ Utility Vehicle is a compact all-terrain work vehicle. "All-terrain" means different kinds of land. Gators don't need paved roads. The Gator can ride up and down steep hills or across rocky dirt or muddy fields. The Gator helps the farmer with small and big jobs.

Take a ride

Some families use Gators to deliver lunch to the farmers in far-off fields.

Heavy duty

A Gator can carry heavy loads, like these bags of fertilizer.

Special delivery

Gators deliver tubs of feed from the silo to the cows in the barn.

Working hard

Gators haul tools and wood to repair fences. Heavy fenceposts, used to keep animals in and hungry **predators** out, can also be carried by the Gator.

FUN FACT

Gators are used to smooth the dirt on many Major League Baseball fields in the United States.

The farm at night

The farm is still busy after the sun sets. The farmer uses lights in the barn to care for animals and bright lights on the machines to work the fields. Some farmers even plow the fields at night wearing special night-vision goggles that let them see in the dark!

Bright lights
This farmer uses the lights on the tractor to see where to pull the fertilizer tank.

8:00 P.M. One more weed

n the last remaining light, the farmer walks through the fields for a final check.

10:00 P.M. Always working

The combine uses its bright lights to finish harvesting a wheat field.

MIDNIGHT Wide awake

Some animals, like this barn owl, are awake at night and sleep during the day. They are called **nocturnal**

3:00 A.M. Watch out!

The wolf hunts at night. Strong fences will keep the farm animals safe.

From farm to market to you

Once a farmer has planted and harvested a crop, it is ready to take a trip from the farm to your kitchen table. How does it happen? Let's follow the journey of a peach to find out.

❶ Pick and pack the peaches

Peaches are picked from the trees before they are fully **ripe**, so they don't rot before they get to you. They are carefully packed into crates or boxes.

FUN FACT

Nectarines are peaches without the fuzz.

❷ To market, to market

The farmer's peaches are sold both near the farm and far away.

Near

Many small farms sell their produce at outdoor **farmers' markets**, which are usually near the farms. The fruits and vegetables are fresh because they do not spend time traveling.

Far

The farmer stacks the boxed peaches into **refrigerated trucks** that drive long distances. If you live very far from where peaches are grown, **airplanes** will fly the peaches to you. The peaches must be transported quickly to the refrigerated **produce section** of a supermarket or they will rot, and the farmer won't get any money for his crop.

❸ You buy the peach

Whether in a small roadside market or in an enormous supermarket, you buy the peach and take it home.

Seasons on the farm

The farm is a busy place all year long.

SUMMER

The days of summer are long, hot, and filled with lots of activity. Fruit ripens on the trees and vines, and vegetables poke out from the ground. Farmers pick berries, peaches, tomatoes, cucumbers, lettuce, corn, and peppers and often sell them at roadside stands. In the late summer, farmers drive combines to harvest wheat. Silos are filled with chopped grain for the animals to eat during winter.

Cows in the pasture
The grass grows thick in the summer, giving the cows tasty meals.

FALL

As the air grows cooler and the days become shorter, it's time for the harvest. Pumpkins must be gathered and the apples in the orchard must be picked before the weather turns too cold. The corn is harvested with a combine. Root vegetables, such as potatoes and beets, are ready to be dug up and eaten. After the harvest, farmers till the fields, or turn the soil, to keep it healthy.

WINTER

While the soil rests in the cold weather, farmers get ready for the new year. They plan their crops. They make sure their machines are in tip-top shape. They heap extra straw in the barn to keep the animals cozy. The animals grow thicker coats to keep warm. Some farmers gather the sap from maple trees and chop fallen trees for firewood. Farmers in warmer climates tend to their citrus trees. They work hard to protect their trees from unexpected frosts.

A **lamb** stands on shaky legs only a few minutes after being born.

SPRING

The sun comes out and warms the farm after the winter's chill. Farmers till, plant, and fertilize their fields so their new crops will grow. Flowers bloom, filling the farm with bright color. Cows, horses, and other farm animals return to their pastures to graze. Baby animals are born, and their mothers take care of them, making sure they grow big and strong so they will enjoy many seasons on the farm.

Warm weather farms

Cotton farm

Cotton is a fiber grown on farms. Cotton has been used to make clothing for 5,000 years.

White and fluffy

Cotton bolls are fluffy cotton fibers and seeds.

From plant to T-shirt

❶ Cotton is picked by a **cotton harvester**. The harvester removes all the bolls from the plant and stores them in a large basket behind the driver.

❷ A machine called a **cotton gin** (gin is short for engine) removes the seeds from the bolls and cleans the cotton.

❸ The cotton is sent to a factory and spun into yarn. The yarn is woven into fabric and used to make your clothes.

FUN FACT

Cotton is used to make more than fabric. It is used to make cotton balls, cottonseed oil for salad dressing and margarine, and even dollar bills.

cotton harvester

Peanut farm

The peanut plant originally grew only in South America, but now most peanuts are grown in the southern United States.

Not nuts

Peanuts are not nuts—they are **legumes**. Legumes are vegetables that have pods of seeds with protective coverings. Peas, beans, and lentils are also legumes.

FUN FACT

If you are the average kid, you will eat 1,500 peanut butter and jelly sandwiches before you graduate from high school.

Underground peg

When a peanut plant grows, bright yellow flowers appear first. Then a stem, also called a **peg**, grows from the flower and curves downward and pushes into the soil. Seed pods, which are the peanuts in the shell, grow on the peg, underground.

Pineapple farm

Pineapples are tropical fruits grown in Hawaii, the Caribbean, Asia, and South America.

A long time

Most fruits take three to four months to grow. A pineapple takes 18 months. Pineapples are not grown from seeds. They are grown from the tops, or **crowns**, of other pineapples.

Did You Know?

The fruit was named pineapple because European explorers thought the outside looked like a pine cone and the inside looked like an apple.

Cold weather farms

Christmas tree farm

Christmas trees are harvested in the weeks and days before Christmas, but farmers carefully tend to these crops for years and years, from seedlings to full-grown trees.

Pruning

The farmer trims the branches with **pruning shears** to give them their triangular shape.

Rows of trees

Christmas trees are planted in rows. They take eight to 12 years to grow. Christmas trees are **evergreens**. This means they stay green all year long.

Christmastime

In November and December, farmers cut down the trees that are ready and wrap them up to be sold in time for Christmas.

Cranberry bog

Cranberries grow on low vines in wet, sandy fields called **bogs**. They are harvested in the northern United States.

FUN FACT

Farmers use a "bounce test" to see if a cranberry is good or bad. Cranberries have pockets of air inside them. If a cranberry is spoiled or damaged, it will not bounce.

Dry harvest

For the dry harvest, a special machine that looks like a lawn mower picks the cranberries off the vines. The cranberries that are not bruised are bagged and sold as whole cranberries.

Wet harvest

Farmers flood the bog. Special machines drive through the water and knock the berries off the vines. The berries float to the top of the water and are gathered up. These cranberries will be made into juice, sauce, or breads.

Maple syrup farm

Maple syrup comes from the **sap** of maple trees. Sap is a sweet, sticky liquid inside a tree.

Collecting sap

Small farms collect the sap by drilling a **spigot** or a tap into the trunk of a tree. The sap drips out of the tap and into a bucket. Larger farms use machines that suck the sap from the tree like a vacuum. Then the sap is boiled until it turns into syrup.

FUN FACT

Pure maple syrup does not freeze solid at cold temperatures. It just gets thicker.

spigot

Farms around the world

Chocolate farm

Chocolate comes from the **cacao bean**, which is grown on the west coast of Africa and in South America. First, the beans are picked. Then, they are dried in the sun and roasted. Next, they are mashed into a thick cream called **cocoa butter**. Cocoa butter is very bitter, so a lot of sugar must be added to it before it becomes sweet chocolate.

cacao bean

Rice farm

Rice is a grain, like wheat or barley. Farmers grow rice in **paddies**—fields flooded with water. Rice is harvested either by hand or by a machine called a **rice harvester**. Sometimes if the rice paddies are on a hillside, they are **terraced**, or made to look like stairs. This way the water does not run down the hill and wash away the crop.

Ostrich farm

Ostriches are big birds that cannot fly. Farmers raise ostriches for their skin, meat, eggs, and feathers. Ostrich skin is used to make shoes, coats, and purses. Ostrich feathers are sometimes used in feather boas. Ostrich farms are found in New Zealand, Australia, South Africa, and the United States.

coffee plant

coffee beans

Coffee farm

Coffee is made from the beans of the coffee tree. After the beans are picked, they are roasted. Coffee is grown in South America, Africa, and other warm climates, such as Jamaica and Hawaii.

All for you

Farms near and far grow many of the everyday things you use, from the food you eat to the clothes you wear, and even the paper in the book you're reading right now. Visit a farm and see for yourself!

Photo credits

The publisher would like to thank the following for their kind permission to reproduce their photographs:

ABBREVIATIONS KEY: t-top, b-bottom, r-right, l-left, c-center, a-above, f-far, bkgd-background, bo-border

Cover images
Front David Frazier/Corbis; Keith Weller/USDA(tr); Catalinus/Dreamstime.com(tl)
Back Image Source/Corbis
6-7 David Frazier/Corbis
8-9 Keith Weller/USDA(8c); Qiwoman01/Dreamstime.com(9tr); Erikdegraaf/Dreamstime.com(9lb); Bill Tarpenning/USDA(9cb); Ken Hammond/USDA(9br)
10-11 Sue/Shutterstock, Inc.(bkgd); Tony Campbell/Shutterstock, Inc.(10l); Jack Shiffer/Dreamstime.com(10r); Little Blue Wolf Productions/Corbis(11tl); Elena Elisseeva/Shutterstock, Inc.(11tr); Andy Kazie/Dreamstime.com(11bl); Gregory Johnston/Big Stock Photo(11br)
12-13 Francisco Amaral Leitao/Shutterstock, Inc.(12tfl); Ecobo/Dreamstime.com(12tl); Martin Bowker/Fotolia(12tr); Tom Oliveira/Fotolia(12tfr); Mikhail Tolstoy/Fotolia(13tfl); Javier Soto Vazquez/Big Stock Photo(13tl); John Carleton/Fotolia(13tr); Yuri_Arcurs/Fotolia(13tfr); Tim McCabe/USDA(13b)
14-15 goborut/Image Vortex(bkgd); Victorburnside/Dreamstime.com (bo); Dana/Dreamstime.com(14t); Tomislav Stajduhar/Fotolia(14bl); Dan Collier/Shutterstock, Inc.(14bc); MitarArt/Shutterstock, Inc.(14br); Cre8tive Images/Shutterstock, Inc. (15bl); matt/Shutterstock, Inc.(15bc)

16-17 David P. Smith/Shutterstock, Inc.(bkgd)
18-19 Philip Coblentz/Brand X/Corbis (18); Emmanuelle Guillou/Fotolia (19b)
24-25 Disorderly/Dreamstime.com (25b)
26-27 Angelo Gilardelli/Dreamstime.com(26b); bg_knight/Dreamstime.com(27tr); Red2000/Dreamstime.com(17bl); Ian Klein/Dreamstime.com(27bc); Jupiterimages/BrandX/Corbis (27br), Leonid Nyshko/Dreamstime.com(27bkgd)
28-29 Vasko Miokovic/iStockphoto (c); Iwka/Dreamstime.com(28t); Blaz Kuie/Shutterstock, Inc.(28c); Olga Shelego/Big Stock Photo (28c); Thomas Brostrom/Big Stock Photo(28c); Carmen Martinez Banus/iStockphoto(28b); Christine Bladeras/iStockphoto(29b)
30-31 Joe Gough/Shutterstock, Inc.(bkgd); Martine Wagner/Fotolia (30c); Uschi Hering/Fotolia(30r); Martin Bowker/Fotolia(31l); hhood/CanStockPhoto(31c); Tyler Olsen/Shutterstock, Inc.(31r)
32-33 Arne Thaysen/iStockphoto (32); Ken Hammond/USDA(33bl); Bob Snook/ShutterPoint(33tc); Cheryl Kunde/Fotolia(33c); Donald Gruener/iStockphoto(33r)
34-35 freaksmg/Dreamstime.com (34c); Olga Aleksandrovna Lisitskaya/Big Stock Photo(34b); Victoria Short/Big Stock Photo(34b); Paul Cowan/Big Stock Photo(34b); Norman Chan/Big Stock Photo(34b); Suzannah Skeleton/iStockphoto (34b); Lana Langlois/Stutterstock, Inc.(34b); Henryk Dybka/Fotolia(35l); Ariel Bravy/Shutterstock,Inc.(35br)
36-37 Chris H. Galbraith/Shutterstock, Inc.(bo); David Frazier/Corbis(36); 2windspa/CanStockPhoto(37l); Shawn Hine/Fotolia(37tr); Eyewire/Getty Images/Punchstock(37br)

38-39 ScottBauer/USDA(38); Lorna/Dreamstime.com(39tl); Hallgard/CanStockPhoto(39cr); erinrenee/CanStockPhoto(39bl)
40-41 Piotr Sikora/Fotolia(bo); Brand X Pictures/JupiterImages (bkgd); Randy Lorance/ShutterPoint (40); John Vachon/USDA(41tl); Andrew Furst/ShutterPoint(41tr); Justyna Furmanczyk/Shutterstock, Inc.(41b)
42-43 Hannah Cleghorn/Shutterstock, Inc.(bo); Andrew Ivanov/Shutterstock, Inc.(bo); Stephen Ausmus/USDA(bkgd); Jupiter Images/Matton(42); jezebella/CanStockPhoto(43tl); Albert Opveiga/Dreamstime.com (43c); Teruhiko Mori/Shutterstock, Inc.(43br)
44-45 David Frazier/Corbis(bkgd); Keith Weller/USDA(44l); Simple Stock Shots/Punchstock(44r); Bryan Ledgard/ShutterPoint(45c); Markowski/Dreamstime.com(45r)
46-47 Shaun Lowe/iStockphoto (bkgd); Bill Tarpenning/USDA(46); Monica Perkins/iStockphoto(47tr,tl); Marcel Pelletier/iStockphoto(47br); Diane Diedrich/iStockphoto(47bl); Lana Langlois/Shutterstock, Inc.(47br)
48-49 Kurt/Dreamstime.com(48c); Doug Wilson/USDA(49tl); Cristi Matei/Shutterstock, Inc.(49br); Keith Weller/USDA(49l)
50-51 Photodisc(51cr)
52-53 Ingram Publishing(53tl); Design Pics Inc.(53tr); Eric Gevaert/Shutterstock, Inc.(53bl); Heinz Effner/Big Stock Photo(53br)
54-55 Leonid Nishko/Shutterstock, Inc.(54bkgd); Francisco Amaral Leitao/Shutterstock, Inc.(54l); Andrew F. Kazmierski/Shutterstock, Inc.(54r); Bill Tarpenning/USDA (55tl); Robert Pernell/Fotolia(55tr); analiza/Fotolia(55bfl); Stephen Galvin/ShutterPoint(55bl)
56-57 Morris Photo Images/ShutterPoint(56cl); Charanya

Girish/ShutterPoint(56bl); Jorge Casais/ShutterPoint(56tr); Darrell Fifield/ShutterPoint(56br); Ron Hilton/Shutterstock, Inc.(57l); Eric Gevaert/Fotolia(57tr); Petr Nad/Fotolia(57cr); Elena Elisseeva/Shutterstock,Inc.(57br)
58-59 Albo/Dreamstime.com (58bkgd); rgbspace/Dreamstime.com(58c); Scott Rothstein/Fotolia(58bl); Dana Heinemann/Shutterstock, Inc. (59bkgdt); Marc Dietrich/Shutterstock, Inc.(59tl); Eugene Bocharev/Shutterstock, Inc. (59bkgdb); Lisa F. Young/Shutterstock, Inc.(59b)
60-61 Jason Tench/Shutterstock, Inc.(bkgdl); Stephen Pierce/ShutterPoint(bkgdc); Christy Thompson/Shutterstock, Inc.(bkgdr); Rob Parker/Big Stock Photo(60tc); Lori Sparkia/Shutterstock, Inc.(60cl,c); Janos Gehring/Shutterstock, Inc. (60bc); Eileen Mayer/Big Stock Photo(60bl); Keith Weller/USDA (61cl); Graca Victoria/Shutterstock, Inc.(61tr); Rick Parsons(61br)
62-63 supri jono suharjoto/Fotolia (62tl); Robert Churchill/iStockphoto (62cl); javarman/Stockxpert(62c); Tzjaczkowski/Dreamstime.com (62cr); Danny Smythe/Fotolia(62br); Xavier Marchant/Fotolia(63tl); Matka Wariatka/Fotolia(63cl); Karens4/ Dreamstime.com(63c); Irina Tischenko/Fotolia(63bc); Cartesia(bkgd)
64 arius/Stockxpert

All other images © Deere & Company.

Every effort has been made to trace the copyright holders of photographs, and we apologize if any omissions have been made.